B U R N

Allison Adelle Hedge Coke

with illustrations by
Dustin Illetewahke Mater

MadHat Press
Asheville, North Carolina

MadHat Press
MadHat Incorporated
PO Box 8364, Asheville, NC 28814

This special edition is provided with permission courtesy of Coffee House Press (Streaming). Portions of this work have additionally been published in *Anti–*, *Ghost Town*, and *Caliban*.

The Library of Congress has assigned
this edition a Control Number of
2017900328

ISBN 978-1-941196-45-8 (paperback)

Cover art and interior illustrations by Dustin Illetewahke Mater
Cover design by Marc Vincenz
Book design by MadHat Press

www.MadHat-Press.com

First Printing

Other Works by Allison Hedge Coke

Poetry

The Year of the Rat
Dog Road Woman
Off-Season City Pipe
Blood Run
Streaming

Memoir

Rock, Ghost, Willow, Deer

As Editor

Sing: Poetry from the Indigenous Americas
Effigies
Effigies II

for the Marfans, for my father

It was a wave of fire
      —Gary Mitschke, *Big Bend Now*

BURN

Cattle carcass still steaming,
                                     roadside   each way   black,
all we can hope is no human's-gone-pugilistic attitude

shrink-posing for fight when air
                                       drains from muscles
through pores evaporating mist in the heat of it

the burnside tangling flesh/ash
                                     through whirlwinds
black plumes, threading time disappearing into dark energy

encapsulating West Texas Border Patrol,
                                     game wardens, smokejumpers'
interior exit, camouflaged,   must outfox the hustle of fire, bustle

whole depletion into retreat, flee, surrender. Surrender.

Hot metal searing Dad's eye,

          soldering pipe flash

into sclera surrounding insight.

          He called to me for water.

I could walk then, but was too

          young to explain.

Knew the serious nature of it,

          how to draw water to heal.

Knew how to handle,

          when passing consumed cattle steaming

their bodies still bearing passing life, still bearing full weight

near normal, flash-burned when

          they could not escape

tumultuous wind-driven flame. Black clouds on scorched earth

managing weather, amassing AEP

          restoration process in the lean

charred leg, delineating linear directions, compass needles,

articulating line of duty death,

            Goins gone, his land still smoking.

Allison Adelle Hedge Coke

The East St. Louis child calling,

                    "Let me out. Let me out!"
as his grandmother's home buckled inward

                        too far gone.

Twice prior, two cousins, sisters lost

                    in fires years before burn
strangling through the family, bit by bit. As if Missouri tornados

weren't wet enough, the fires fueled there, still hardy, taking.

Up river, season error snowmelt maddening levees,   taking
houses in laps
                    long overgrown, smacking them into tinder

somewhere heated, but now there is the quickened confluence
beating away anything substantial
                to vehicle flow, with amorous

waves rolling wide, gyrating revolve, pushing, turning twist
into

back into blaze, the only water deep
              and drifting, not enough hoses
or people to put this out, now another's popped up, maybe more.

By the sixth, caution translates to which way the wind blows,   by
eleventh, homes are temporary, expendable,
                                   nothing matches life.

Massive range-riddling smolder. Tufts turn upward, rise on sweeps.
Glowing bluffs distant horizon, closer
                              burn backs off befuddled

men, women, wishing for work in a heated ten-mile open wide
volcano mouth, held open since seas
                              slid down, lava formed high

not two hundred miles from Carlsbad where evacuations loom,
bats scatter, all wide deep of it,
                              catacombed, put it out north too,

under Los Alamos crazed nuclear weaponry, plutonium storage
experiments hauled over something
                              byway Santa Fe, city

current remnant flagged in trade cloth waving red, yellow flames
on downtown wheeled armadas, honking,
                              "L-e-t u-s o-u-t!" while winds

wind themselves into imperiled   charts, pictographs, cartography cut
loose from Bandolier-sashed mountains,

                      the pockets pushed out

into ashes all around. Now, here, javelinas

                      hurl themselves under
roadside culverts, taking lower pathways from fiery sear.

Remember back on Ridge, fires? Crystal called her sister, Faith said,
                    "The house is gone, all of it."
Sarah standing on top, a black & white in her right palm, her hair

in her left, all of it smoldering.
                    Where's the cat?   My own brother
burning new construction insulation, for the thrill of it; at eight, "Pyromania,"

they said, but never mentioned when he self-immolated at eleven,
no, never gave him that, just coughed
                    away memory of our sister

pouring alcohol on the hard tile, spelling out,
                    "Die Die Die" to
shock us coming home. Kids' stuff.
                    Or, construction workers stubbing

cigarettes into dry grass behind our place,
                    how we burned our rubber
soles stamping while they laughed at us, Mom and Dad burned

their palms putting it out,   ashed,   or her hair shocked that way, white.

13

Allison Adelle Hedge Coke

Glass bottle fire, smokes up crossroads, no
                                            no fiddles found their bow
play   on strings popping alongside road tar
                                                    heels, hollowed ditches full

Russian thistles' bitter scorch, flying out
                                          skeletal-like, running.
Insides turning out, twisting up like lead turns turning. Rising

mantle vapor smoking sunset, rise,
                                     all through night, all through
cooked fields, calves scrambled on, too fast, too fast, the burn. Burn.

We're still missing one hundred twenty-five head
from Rock House Fire.
Seventy-four from the leased Poor Farm land. Neighbors keep

a lookout, nothing. Black Angus, aoudad, pronghorns torched up
like marshmallow roasts, giving tongue
lapped licks on lips curled

quick in heat.   Twenty-nine special Rangers seek the rest, any loose
herds made clean of it. Rustlers, must be.
No vultures vortexed

sight overhead, no buzzards' contours,   no, only smoke belies.

15

Downtown, some fliers offer reward next to a ma and pop chiding
their eldest over dropping lit butt into pathways.
                                             No room for
accidents in *No Country for Old Men*. No room for it where Woody
wore belts decked out by Graybeal, by
                                             Moonlight's best gemstone,
Marfa agate. Too bad the shots didn't display
                                             the cut of them. Real
beauties over sterling silver plate. Now heat plates on low-profile sports

cars tinder prairie grass ignition, cactus wrath. Anything's
at risk; everything's to blame.

Flames following wind the way

water follows wave, over seabed

ground pummeled high, mile
high elevation, sure as Denver, but desert scene. Chihuahuan

and Sonoran, now both carry largest wildfires in colonial
history, both heated harder, spreading

further, than pictured

in recent times. Everything from Tucson through Texas a rage.

Ladybird's roadside flowers billow dust, chocolate
flowers still scenting straight paths familiar.

It's the fury fell

here. Fuming every angle, hopping asphalt,
by the time Gage
Holland breaks from roadside rest area, Hwy. 90 is shut down clean

to Marfa, no one there holds much hope,
Rock House said
to be still smoldering.   It's all without mercy, without peace.

MMXVI

Dreams come easily branded, but no iron rod season's
coming this round. Come easily into
                            infused chicken   games,

forearms stubbed, spoons cooked in dosage blues, shooting
burns, shoot-up euphoria, hero flying
                            through blistered skies,
they called it horse at import, now horses shot, nine of them.
Nerves so frayed teakettle copper melts blue,
                          then white, ash

covered the electric burner on stove range, while the range
outside roared, spat sideways onto
                          roofs, roads, ranches.

Population too sparse here for national concern, no, though
public radio does spare lives nearby, maybe
our own, measly thrill

a bitter bitter thing in coverage accolades, but dammit they do
deserve attention, we depend on them.
Give them glory, we'll

share in it, same face, Border Patrol/Walk In, all phoenix rise,
nothing sheared shares grace,
black peel crusts everything,

surviving's the only reason. Look at it, gone. No fire climax
pines here to justify so much loss,
rebirth here, a fought thing.

Mr. Spanish buried ceremonially in shoebox, under glory, flagpoled,
each niña entered escuela.

Allison Adelle Hedge Coke

It's rough country. Aftermath, don't add up.
                              Logic's subjective.
That's life out here, not much gussy ghost propositions. Trains

all that ever run on time, rest of the clockwork's *when it need*
be business. Rain's only thing missing.
                              When it teases,

lightning sparks whatever's left, six sparks spread within an evening.
By morning smoke's on the plate again.
                              Coexistence only calm.

We expect plunther, plunther along the world's edge, horizon.
One day a rim fire burns so great its whirl will create weather,

        pattern vortices tilt horizontal to vertical, hurling

branch, limb, whatever fills to vorticity. Scorched pathways leaving earth.

All roads travel onward, until they end.
Everything ends in time.
Everything temporary. An eternal fire holds itself, only in heat,

fuel, oxygen, triangulate combustion,
tetrahedral support planes
existence, life spark, yet fire has been carried, cultivated, cured

since first fire. It's log bundle, hollowed, fed.

He fed the first from his pick up on I-44. Tossed the news out his window,
flaming until half of Luther
left Oklahoma in fury so hot, all it left was white ash, the whole of it
under skies dark with night
shining proof of other worlds. Orion holding up east. The gleam of it maddening.

Allison Adelle Hedge Coke

Stars surely shine. Sun's running sky each morning.
Sirius still rounds night except

                                        for seventy days or so.

Always will. Stardust precedes Earth.

Dust here kicks up heavy, towered seventy feet high
in Lubbock years back.
                              High in Arizona now, where

Wallow breaks records like gangbusters.
                              Mainstreamers
picking up haboob as if comprehension made it new.

Predate dust. You can't. Dust has been and rises when-
ever wind wills.

Gusts a given out here.

Where a heat plate scrapes grass like armadillo shell
tears into straw with friction, sparks it,

whole thing burns

bright, spreads for miles in short order. Spreads for miles.

People unable to move through it, leave everything they love, hope
until return, then weep. Like the mother

whose kids shared our

school. One tied to the couch and burned alive after Demerol

downed him there. Bad deal.
Bad deal all over. Drug wars

never won. Border blasting happening here.

Bad deal all over.

SBI burned down the shooting gallery back when. Now
'tis anyone's game, gamble,

                    crap shoot, loosing lives like

spit on clay, baked hard, broken.

                    What's the seed of it?   Crack?

Char rounds out horizon now,
                              used to be shadows. Tall
men in saddles shifting through, now shadow men unsaddled

blow away in wind on giant flat.
                              Secrets untold shudder
what should be proper, what should be here, gone. Gone.

MMXVI

Char brings looseness, holds memory intangible, blackened
earth,　　　 its own beauty, not hollow,
　　　　　　　　　　　　　but kept there. In

evening, vultures scan space, seeking remnant, passing cranes feast
on roasted grasshoppers, crickets, larva.
　　　　　　　　　　　　In morning, phoenix

rises through community sight, open to opportunity, lamenting.
We come here hoping for more,
　　　　　　　　　　　　knowing nothing surprises

those who present hope. What is hope?　　　　Feel fortune?
Opportunity? Grace?

In the meantime, all wade through ashes, in a place ash
turned to stone when volcanoes

came up from the sea floor,
now high desert, what's left of it, caldera.

Putting down the suffering,
the day's work. Beloved and betrothed—horse, cattle, goat.

The chickens hold a roost with their burnt legs, they go as well
to wayside memory, now asunder,

memory, like the paisano,
skipping in, out, walking upward, falling,

bird, fountain motion,
moving.

We were born here, someone mentions.

We don't know when fire will still, when embers left end themselves,
nor when rain will visit, come to renew,
$$\text{to free us from burn, from danger.}$$

Nor do we know what caused this end, the timing of a heat plate on long
grass, the nearness of glass to blade in sunlight.
$$\text{The year of the drought,}$$

though some speculate larger cycles,
$$\text{the roundabout here is intangible.}$$

Nor do we offer ideas, unless plied with cold lager in the heat here, or

in evenings laid out under fiery stars still gleaming, always lighting
pathways we lean toward in nighttime escapes,
$$\text{to towns down the road.}$$

No we don't know. All we know is we are not alone
and yet we are and everything is subject to fire,
$$\text{even water leaves}$$

35

in heated paths. What we don't know we don't search for, nor do we attempt to understand. No, we take it.

Deal with it. We muster.

We move through the crust salvaging pieces, we are salvagers, moving
through the heat, lifting recognizable source,

> lifting permanence

from tempered time. Lifting home. We tote burned wire, curled it into sphere
like story, surround light with it,

> harness energy and plug it in until

spherical globes rekindle Marfa fires once surrounding livestock, now bordering
glow, it is the strand we fill, the obligation,

> remaking stuff from cinder.

Remaking.

Remaking.

   Twins we carried then laid.

         One light, one fire.   Do they rest?
Do they feel this burden? The melting iron, wire,

               shifting wind funneling

them across prairie in winding plumes, are they turning?

               What of the way
we embraced to conceive them?   Held there like satchels beaded

in cedar sprig holding floral bursts.   In dense trees, hills,   waterways
we come from   the kneel there

            when we bury, bring them gifts, make offerings.

In the burn of your brow, when you hastened, did you think before belting
me? Conceive intent?

         What were you, but burning?

         What were you,   but burning?

39

Yet, fire is the birth of life, the spark there and we

were with spark, ignited.

My life emptied into the banks below mounds they now lay within. They

were within me, now within our mother.

I sometimes long to lie there but

I, too, muster.

You,   long gone to other worlds,

                not over there, but wandering spark,

                          burn.

Full download of the album *Streaming*, including Burn from the Rd Klā project with music by Kevin Bell and Laura Ortman and vocal rendition by Allison Adelle Hedge Coke, is available with the purchase of this book, or the poetry collection *Streaming* from Coffee House Press.

Enter the code: fH6k7NmR at soundtrax.com to receive courtesy of Long Person (Yvwi Gvnahita) Records.

Acknowledgements and appreciation:

To the Lannan Foundation for bringing me to this unexpected work at Marfa.

Thank you to Dustin Mater for the stunning and meaningful illustrations.

Thank you to Kelvyn Bell and Laura Ortman for the genius music on the Rd Klā project album, *Streaming*.

Thank you to Coffee House Press for accepting *Streaming* and supporting the idea of this special edition, and for supporting the making of the music.

Thank you to Marc Vincenz and MadHat Press for the place to realize this selection.

This book is dedicated to the survivors of the Marfa fires, to all the lost in all these fires raging throughout my life and surrounding residency in something miraculous, maddening, and mediating.

To those who still suffer from the damage there and before.

To my brother, Walter, my sister, Steph,

to Faith, Crystal, and Sarah,

the kids we heard about down the road and

the kids we went to school with who perished in fires,

and those twins we laid, those twins—

About the Author

Allison Adelle Hedge Coke's books include *Streaming, Blood Run, Off-Season City Pipe, Dog Road Woman, Sing: Poetry from the Indigenous Americas, Effigies, Effigies II, and Rock, Ghost, Willow, Deer.* Awards include an American Book Award, King*Chavez*Parks Award, Lifetime Achievement Award Native Writers Circle of the Americas, Wordcrafter of the Year Award, Pen Southwest Book Award, and the 2016 Library of Congress Witter Bynner Fellowship. She is founding faculty for the VCFA MFA in Writing & Publishing program, and a Distinguished Professor of Creative Writing at the University of California Riverside. Hedge Coke is mixed heritage, raised in North Carolina, Canada, and on the Great Plains.

ABOUT THE ARTIST

DUSTIN ILLETEWAHKE MATER, Chickasaw, is an award-winning multimedia artist and designer. He was the first southeastern tribal member to be a part of Pendleton Blankets Legendary Collection, and has a shell gorget housed in the permanent collection at the Smithsonian's National Museum of the American Indian (NMAI) in Washington, D.C., with additional artistic works shown in Paris, Edinburgh, the National Parks Service, and multiple reputable galleries. Mater has won numerous awards, including first place in sculpture at Santa Fe Indian Market. Mater previously illustrated *Spider Brings Fire* by Linda Hogan.

CPSIA information can be obtained
at www.ICGtesting.com
Printed in the USA
BVOW05s0337110118

504943BV00010B/88/P